How to Build a Professional Sales Career
Preparation and Demonstration
Sell <u>Anything to Anyone</u>

Increase Confidence, Excitement, and Profit

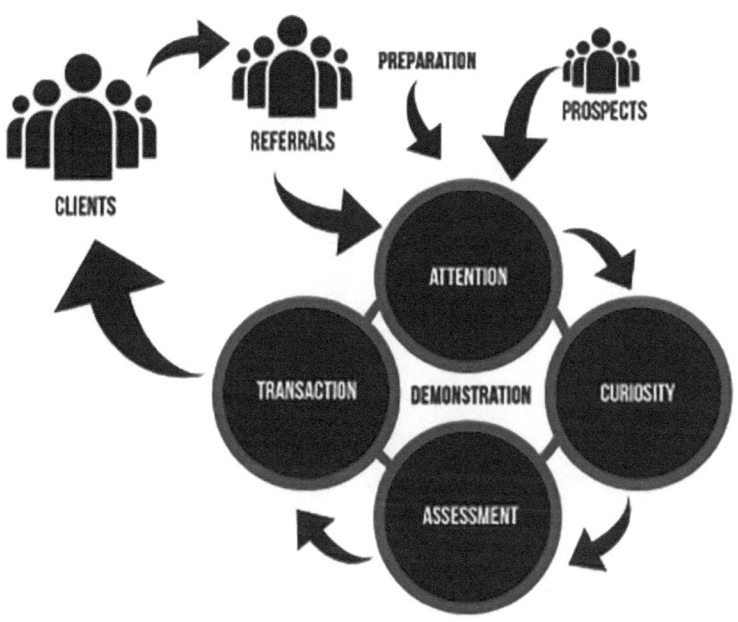

Gold File; make sales from NO's / better contacts more sales.
ABC (always be closing)
Richard L Erickson C.Ht. professional sales trainer

Table of Contents

PREFACE

Whether new, a seasoned veteran or just someone who wants to improve your interaction skills, this manuscript is packed full of sales information, methods, and building blocks to success. To make this book easy to absorb, I have divided the data into two sections; Preparation and Demonstration.

Preparation: The chapters within this section focus on background knowledge, which is needed to become proficient in developing your sales skills. Preparation includes throwing out the garbage, staying positive with goals and habits, knowing the nomenclature of a sale, and features within your product.

Demonstration : The second section of this book is devoted to communication, call scripts, my GOLD File, procedures, phases, presentation, transactions, client building, and referrals.

As you travel through the chapters, you will encounter perception by observation. As salespeople, we must understand that what we observe and perceive may be utterly different from that of our potential client. To better explain how we view observation and perception, let me offer an analogy.

Fishing can be a prolonged and enjoyable process. Floating along in a gently rocking boat, as the sun warms the skin. The sounds of gulls are chatting while gliding effortlessly overhead; this is the case Utopia.

Until, that is, you are fishing for survival. Now the experience takes on an entirely new standpoint. The gulls are frightening the fish. The sun is driving the fish deeper and slowing their eating habits. The boat looks like a predator, moving the fish farther away, and your hunger grows as, for the second day, you're finding it harder to catch a meal.

Perception and observation are crucial to determining your thought patterns, and how you arrange these patterns to assure success. I designed this book to allow you to gain an epiphany (defined as an experience which causes a sudden and striking realization).

Within *How to Build a Professional Sales Career*, we will explore various characteristics of the sale from different angles. We will compare a sales career to other occupations, study background building blocks, observe a new collection of formats, features, scripts, proposals, and presentations. My goal is for the reader to experience such an epiphany as you acquire the basics and new ideas, then suddenly, a realized thought—and bang there it is. Selling in smooth fluid motion simple and easy—working smarter, not harder.

SECTION 1
Preparation

Chapter 1

Begin by Throwing Out the Garbage

Training since birth

You have been training to be a sales professional since birth. From the first interactions between you and your caregiver, selling was innocently voiced. As a baby, you signaled wants (food, play, teething, dirty diapers) with verbal and nonverbal commands (selling) that your caregiver satisfied. Your caregiver then, using verbal and nonverbal commands, (selling) taught you the fundamentals of life's rules. As you grew older, selling and buying became entwined in a network of life's objects and services, like toys wanted, likes and dislikes of foodstuffs, learning new ideas, playing, making friends, sports, school, clothes, first car, odd jobs, deciding your future, dating—get the picture?

This book will help you develop a blueprint for success that will enhance your sales skills. As you become a top-tier selling professional, you will be in high demand in several wide-open sales fields of your desire, harvesting the rewards. Next, let us throw out the garbage.

Negative Perceptions

It is essential to clear your mind of certain per-conceived philosophies, suggestions, techniques, and contrary views concerning sales because we can never assume anything when interacting with the public. Even though most readers of this book are in sales, I am starting as if you are at the beginning of your career looking forward to a vocation in sales.

The general public's opinion of most salespeople is negative. So, it only stands to reason that FEAR of REJECTION is the biggest drawback in the minds of most in, or contemplating, the sales industry. Also, why not? Fear and rejection are two of the harshest emotions we humans face. Negative opinions should be different thoughts when you consider that all goods and services travel through sales from the raw material to the finished product and salespeople are involved with every step along the way. So why the cynical view? The answer is four-fold:1. NO, is directed at the salesperson, 2. Disgrace, within the sales profession 3. False perception of inadequate training, and 4. Procrastination.

- **NO, is directed at the salesperson:** Salespeople often get frustrated when making prospect calls, partly because most salespeople haven't learned proper phone technique, and up to 85% of cold calls say no. When we investigate the procedure, there can be many reasons a contact gives you a *NO* answer, i.e., they are sick, lousy timing, lost job, kids are fighting, neighbor or serviceman just rang the doorbell, a sick pet, or unexpected expenses. These are a few of the reasons people might say no to your call. Keep in mind that the rejection is *not* directed at you. I repeat not directed at you. In chapter 11, I will show you how to change a NO to GOLD.

- **Disgrace:** There is a long-standing, on-going belief that sales positions are only for those born with a gift for gab, are pushy and have significant ego problems. Disgrace is probably the biggest misconception in the sales industry.

- **False perception of inadequate training:** The first-year turn-over rate is 40%, and numerous positions go unfilled. Turnover and vacant positions are due to the misconceptions of the sales industry, not inadequate training.

- **Procrastination:** Is a human trait that puts off doing a task until the last minute or not at all. Most of us occasionally procrastinate when a job is hard or unruly. Therefore, naturally, salespeople tend to lean in that direction when confronted with tough projects. When procrastination, disgrace, and the belief that a NO answer is directed towards the salesperson, one can understand why the turnover rate and unfilled positions occur.

Understanding these negative opinions, we can appreciate why new and average salespeople lose 25% of all sales, just because they procrastinate and didn't follow up promptly. These same salespeople fill their daily routines with non-productive work, spending on average only one-third of their daily activity talking to potential buyers, and nearly 6 in 10 salespeople (60%) don't change their routine even after they find out what works (true procrastination).

As readers of this Book; let us make a pledge. "I will throw out the garbage by discarding fear, rejection, a NO response is directed at me, disgrace, false perception of inadequate training, and procrastination. I will concentrate on the qualities of a successful sales professional who takes their work schedule seriously, attends multiple training courses, is humble, honest, trustworthy, observant, likable, well-spoken, knowledgeable, and has the best interest of the prospect in mind."

Chapter 2

Sales Professionals Wanted

When I began my sales career, I was a newly married adult looking to make some money. I quickly learned that if I wanted to be successful, I needed help. So, I turned to a sales professional in our office who had been in the trenches, made good money, had fun, and made selling look simple and easy.

I used his winning techniques as my primary sales platform. As I became more sales proficient, I added personal strategies and eventually surpassed my mentor. I'll never, however, forget his help. He gave me an edge. I was ahead of the game. This book will provide you with that same edge and help you become a leader in your sales field by tying the past with the present.

Man, for thousands of years, has used basic sales techniques to barter for goods and services. With business expansion worldwide, the word "barter" gave way to salesmanship. In the last sixty years, our agricultural and industrial communities have added the technological age that brought into existence numerous websites, blogs, search engines, online seminars, and eBooks, using new systems, keywords, and phrases to aid salespeople.

New terminology, however, has a downside that could sabotage a sales procedure by putting human interaction in the shadows, over complicating the process, and making it harder for the sales professional and prospective client to ask, which methods are trustworthy?

As the author, with over 40 years of experience selling tangible and intangible products, I feel qualified to answer your questions.

I would say read. Read everything you can get your hands on but use this book as your foundation; a floor to build your perpetual sales career around.

Stepping Stones

There are many vocations to examine when entering the job market, each having a full learning curve. A small sprinkling of occupations among all, teacher, secretary, laborer, store clerk, waitress, physician, business owner, professor, attorney, car salesperson, accountant or millwright, starts out on a somewhat equal playing field.

Before settling on a career, the average person will spend about twelve years gaining a GED or high school diploma, four more years for an undergraduate degree, and five to seven additional years obtaining a PhD. Along the educational path, most students will be deciding their life's work and taking classes to enhance their goal. Several will increase specific skills by taking countless seminars and training courses.

Most Careers has One Big Pitfall

The pitfall starts early in the career process, even as you enter the workforce. Suddenly and somewhat rudely you are blended within tens of thousands of people that are training for the same position. You find that hundreds have higher GPA scores, more experience, and better references. You look around and see you have become white noise in a field of soloists; just another number in line for one position.

Even if you land a similar position, with growing technology, your job, and even your employer company, may NOT exist in ten to thirty years. Nothing is worse than a sixty-year-old employee, with thirty years' experience, having what is considered "obsolete job experience" and being laid off. Also, downsizing middle management adds to the grief.

Starting in the 1990s, companies around the world, began cutting upper mobility positions. Tesla chief executive Elon Musk wrote, "We are flattening the management structure to improve communication, combining functions where sensible and trimming activities that are not vital to the success of our mission." Downsizing also contributes to slow wage growth even in our robust economic conditions. If it sounds a little scary—IT IS!

You can Avoid the Pitfall

Some professions avoid job loss. Engineers, physicians, corporate attorneys, and supreme court judges, to name a few. However, for most of us, the fear of the pitfall remains tucked away in the back of our minds. A sales position can help silence your fear of that pitfall because it affords numerous individuals an opportunity to control their future.

Every product or service involves multi-stage development. With each stage, there are numerous opportunities for high paying sales professionals. Sales are engaged in every step of product development; raw materials, distribution, wholesale, retail, renewables, resale, and scrap.

As the world's global markets continue to advance, this age-old profession is showing an incredible resurgence. Sales representatives and marketing managers are increasingly in high demand, and so are their income potentials. Whether you have a GED or PhD., the business world is looking for trained salespeople.

Today's leading sales representatives can earn high five, six, and even seven-figure incomes, including great benefit packages. Many companies offer their sales staff full retirement pension benefits with as little as five years seniority. Additionally, companies often pay commissions on renewable payments. A good example is the insurance industry. Called renewals, they arise from the initial insurance policy sale, and each year, as the client renews the policy, a commission is paid. This "side sale" allows for annual income to steadily accumulate, in some cases, for decades (a built-in annuity).

Moreover, if you are recognition-oriented, a sales position can offer opportunities to win trips, bonuses, trophies, and company honors. Finally, job security is sustained with the understanding of your worth to any company you wish to pursue.

From Scary to Excitement and Confidence

A 2017 Alexander Group survey showed that sales growth has steadily increased by 5% over the last five years and this growth is expected to grow by an additional 2% in 2018. If there are products made, sales professionals will be in high demand.

According to a 2016 survey by MarketWatch, businesses of all types, from mom-and-pop to multi-billion-dollar industries, are looking for people who can sell, and if you can sell, these companies will train you in their products and features. This same survey looked at the top 10 technology companies and found 126,000 unfilled sales positions for business-to-business salespeople with starting pay ranging from $100,000 to north of $250,000 per year, plus exceptional benefits packages.

Look at the beautiful things a career in sales has to offer. Once you attain the necessary sales skills found in this book along with your acquired education, your sales professionalism is released, and the combination will empower you to Sell Anything to Anybody.

Chapter 3

Do Your Homework

Know the Pay Structure and Terminology

Whatever you do in life, it is imperative to do your homework and make sure your eyes are wide open before making a decision that could plan your life for life. The following will be an excellent start to allowing a salesperson to "kick the tires" before signing on the dotted line:

- Benefits packages: Every company has prior hiring requirements (i.e., education, experience, specific knowledge, geographic location). Understanding your benefits will help you stay within the company's minimum guidelines for success. Benefits usually start with a weekly income; salary, a combination of salary and commission, straight commission, or a siphon that covers supplies. If you find your weekly pay is a straight commission, you will only make money if you make a sale. If your weekly wage is a draw, an advancement against future commission, then you will owe the company, which is paid back as you make future sales. Additionally, is the commission structure a flat amount, or does it increase/decrease as sales quotas or dollar amounts increase or decrease? Are there split commissions, renewals, and overrides? Will you have other benefits? What about your other benefits—medical and disability insurance, 401k, vacation and/or sick pay— and what are the rules to win sales contests and company honors?

- Product Knowledge: 1. Know your industry and the types of people you will be contacting. Understand the verbiage your potential clients use, i.e., if you are going to be a pharmaceutical salesperson, understand the use of certain old and new current medications and their pros and cons. 2. Know the medical language and shortcuts doctors and nurses use to communicate. 3. Know your competitors' products, forward and backward, and how they compare to your product. 4. Know your company's products, the cost structure, price points (wholesale, retail quantity discounts) what they do, all their features, production methods, chemical formulas, shelf life, and warranty.

- Contact List: A list of the following—names, emails, tweets, phone numbers. The importance of knowing where you obtained the sources of your contact list will control the way you approach the sales call. I cannot stress enough your understanding of the where, when, and why of each contact on your list. Were your contacts obtained from a cold call list, a response to an ad, a curiosity response, a referral, an upgrade from a previous sale, renewal, or Gold File (see chapter 11)? Once you divide your contact list into type categories, it is time to proceed to the sales call.

- Sales Call: (talking with a contact) is outbound selling because you are contacting an individual for a face-to-face meeting. Leaving a voice message, email, tweet, or talking to an individual that is not a decision maker "callback" does not count as sales calls. A sales call exists when you have made actual contact with a decision-maker or, in some cases, a group of decision-makers, from your contact list. If the contact answers YES, you now have a potential client (prospect). If your contact says NO, don't get discouraged. A good percentage will be positive once you learn my GOLD File (see Gold File chapter 11). The more you practice each type of call the more you will use the correct "hot button" words and phrases leading to additional and profitable appointments.

- Order-taking: An inbound contact, is an email, call, tweet, or text made to a sophisticated IT device or telemarketer where the buyer calls the company. A growing number of inbound calls involve websites and blogs that offer the respondent gifts. An inbound call to a telemarketer usually takes little sales experience because the prospect is often 95% sold on the product. Unfortunately, companies typically contract telemarketing firms, which in many cases are off-shore firms, where English and Spanish are a foreign languages. Thus, these companies employ script readers, people that learn just enough English or Spanish to read a script and obtain the buyer's name, address, and credit card. Since many telemarketers speak broken English and Spanish and are uneducated about the products offered, they often give salespeople a bad reputation because of the public lumps all salespeople into one group.

- Potential Client: (prospect) A contact becomes a potential client or prospect when there is a positive response from a person or business that shows interest in your product. The potential client can quickly turn into a sales presentation or turn sour if the salesperson does not use proper timing. The presentation date and hour favorable to the potential client, and any necessary paperwork needed to proceed are the two main factors in solidifying the sales presentation.

- Proposal: Any paperwork or visual aid that is used to open the sales presentation. The proposal can be sent, in certain circumstances, ahead of the presentation. Many salespeople use "flip-books" usually within an iPad or other devices in their presentations. The proposal offers the potential client a concentration point and helps the salesperson stay on track.

- Products: The salesperson's items. Products can be tangible (physical objects that can be seen, touched, tested) like cars, appliances, tools, housing. Intangible (non- physical objects purchased for future use) includes insurance, intellectual property, mortgages, and ideas.

- Sales Presentation: A face-to-face meeting with the potential client. During this meeting you, as the salesperson using a sales method, attempt to cause a positive cognitive response such as to induce the buyer to mentally visualize your product that will improve his/her lifestyle; resulting, if done correctly, in a positive transaction (sale).

- Transaction: (close) Exchange of money for a product. A transaction can be positive, negative, or neutral.

  1. Positive transaction: The salesperson convinces the buyer to purchase a product. A SALE

  2. Neutral transaction: The buyer is not satisfied to buy but is still interested and wants to reschedule another appointment. SALE ON HOLD

  3. Negative transaction: The salesperson has not per-suaded the buyer that the product is currently worth more than the sales price. NO SALE

- Client: A person or company that buys a product or service from a salesperson. A salesperson/client relationship only exists after a positive transaction occurs (sale). From the first contact to a client, the salesperson is then paid for his/her efforts. The salesperson can then cultivate the client to help strengthen a sales career with future sales, testimonials, referrals, recommendations, and endorsements.

- Referrals: A contact list of names, phone numbers, emails, or businesses collected from a potential client or client. Referrals are like gold because people have more confidence in doing business with salespeople that have been suggested by friends, neighbors, family or business associates. Is it no wonder the closing ratio is over 80%?

I recommend you gather at least 7 or more referrals from every client. Do the math.

Example: A salesperson acquires 200 sales clients x 7 average referrals = 1400. From these 1400 referrals 60% become sales presentations. 1400 x .60 = 840. With an 80% positive transaction rate 840 x .80 =672 (sales) new clients. Now you have your original 200 clients and 672 new clients. 872 clients to draw future referrals.

Keeping a good salesperson/client relationship with your now 872 clients will pay dividends. If you average just one referral from your original clients and 7 referrals from each new client, you could start off your next year with 4902 new referrals. More referrals than you could see in a year? Imagine your client base in ten years! Again, working smarter, not harder.

Space for Notes

Chapter 4

Metaphor Analogy & Sales Rules

Metaphor and Analogy Energy Amplifiers

The sales professional soon learns that a sales career, although lucrative, requires constant vigor. Conserving energy using the tools of our trade helps keep fatigue at bay, making life more comfortable and fun. Figures of speech, like metaphors and analogies, are two essential tools. The metaphor directly refers to one thing by mentioning another for mental visual effect, and an analogy is two or more metaphors within a parallel story. Psychological visual effects help the astute salesperson to concentrate the potential client's cognitive and emotional thoughts on your proposal and presentation. Cultivating this suggestive mental trick uses the prospective client's energy to desire your product, making the sales more natural.

I will be using metaphors and analogies throughout this handbook. As illustration:

A sales career is an ongoing process. I liken it to rolling a large boulder. Imagine you are assigned a task. Roll a 200lb boulder along a 150 yd footpath in 12 minutes. You could bend over and start slowly pushing the boulder, occasionally stopping to get your breath. It will take a massive amount of energy to get the boulder moving, and when you stop to catch your breath, it will take the same amount of power to get the boulder rolling again while taking the full amount of time to complete your task.

Let's take a different approach to our mission and use a few tools. You could wear a pair of gloves, use a wide strap with two side ropes, and pull the boulder smoothly forward to the goal. Pulling the boulder, using provided tools, will utilize less energy to get the boulder moving, so you will not have to stop and catch your breath, saving you time that allows you to complete your mission within limits.

When we look at each sale and your sales career, it takes significant energy to start, and continued power is required for each developmental step taken along your professional path. However, like the rolling of the boulder, if you use the right tools provided, you will use less energy and have more successes in faster time.

Stay within the Guidelines

If you have played or watched any sport, you understand that there are specific, orderly, and progressive sets of rules. If you break those rules, as many do, there are penalties. A player or players who repeatedly break the rules can lose the game.

In the sales arena, there are also rules, and breaking them could cost you a sale. Stay within the rules and overcome the few penalties we all encounter, and you can make multiple sales. Break too many rules and your out-of-the-game.

The rules of a sales professional occur with verbal, figures of speech, words, and phrases, and the use of nonverbal communication. Rules allow you to know when and what to say, when to be silent, watching your facial and body gestures; listening carefully and responding positively will increase sales. If you are a veteran of sales, revisit your sales industry's vocabulary, goals, and habit-forming procedures to understand and follow the sales procedural progressive steps. It will dramatically increase productivity

Chapter 5

Goals vs. Habits

Goals

Nothing builds confidence better than repeatedly reaching planned goals, and reaching goals creates great selling habits. The definition of a goal is a stated objective that works toward a chosen result within a specific time frame. Goals are formed in the cognitive, logical portion of the brain. Goals are essential to any profession, and sales is no exception. I suggest you start with simple goals that enhance the larger goal.

An example of a larger goal: "I will make the "million dollar round table" in three years." This rather large goal, after a few weeks, might look unattainable, and your confidence and excitement level may weaken and sink. What if you took that goal and broke it down into hours, days, weeks, and months? What if you further calculated these smaller goals by the number of contact calls, to potential client calls, to presentations, and sales, to achieve your larger goal? Throughout the months and years ahead, by steadily reaching each small goal, you will reach your more significant goal within the time limit. Reaching goals will help your excitement and confidence level stay high and intact, holding all together. Goals are also an excellent stepping stone to favorable habit formation.

Habits

Unlike a goal, which is controlled and discarded at will, habits are formed through every day repetitious acts in the older more controlling section of the emotional mid-brain. Once created, a habit is "locked in" and acts automatically. As we age, habits become more and more controlling. Habits, therefore, have seniority over goals. It is crucial to cancel out bad habits and replace them with positive habits, and you can achieve this no matter your sales experience.

In the 1950's a myth about habits was started by Dr. Maxwell Maltz who observed that some of his patients would gain new or changing habits around three weeks after surgery. Even though many scientific experimentation's have since dispelled this myth, many life coaches still claim its existence today. We now know the "mean range" to create a new or change a habit is approximately two months to eight months depending on the person and circumstances, with the "meantime" at 66 days. Don't get frustrated if your habits don't jive with others. Do not fear harmful habits. If you find you have a destructive habit or four that may harm work, replace them by setting goals, listening to defined ideas, reading books that give you alternative sales aids, and taking advice from successful professionals. Give your habits time to change but reinforce them daily.

Habits are life-controlling in many ways, so focus your learning curve on the positives by not filling your head with thoughts that will only lead to fear and rejection. Remember, a habit forms with continuous repetition. Confront it and understand you can change habits and replace them with fresh new positive ones. To show you the importance of forming habits, let's look at this Example:

In sports, teams pay big money to "keep book" on players. Knowing the habits of players can be very beneficial to the opposing team. As a player's habitual traits take over, usually in certain stressful situations, it gives the opposing team a "read." Is the player more apt to go left or right under certain defenses? Does the player throw sidearm or over the top on the three/two pitch? Does the player slide head first or feet first on a close call?

As a salesperson, understand your negative habits and how they automatically kick in under certain circumstances. Next focus on correcting these habits to help control the sales situations; even "read" the buyer. When you can leave fear and rejection in the past where it belongs courage will spring forward and increase closing ratios (sales).

Space for Notes

Chapter 6

Products Overview

Tangible Intangible

As stated in chapter 3, products come in basically two varieties: tangible and intangible. Emotional verbiage and visualization will control most of the presentation with both types.

Tangible products:(physical) Are the touchy-feely type and often purchased for immediate use. An example of tangible products includes computers, software, houses, cars, equipment, boats, furniture, appliances, and tools. The tangible salesperson can implement the emotional imagination by painting mental pictures of the visible product's features, and the logical mind for product demonstration, using logical words and phrases. Focusing on the rational and emotional vocabulary, in coordination, is a potent tandem.

Example: A new home presentation. The realtor can show the buyer each room layout, figure out the placement of their furniture, the appliances, the landscaping, and lighting. The buyer can walk through the house, touch the walls, feel the carpet under their feet, switch on a basement light, run the garage door up and down, and get the feel of this home. The urgency factor is also high because other realtors might be trying to sell the same house. Selling a "sense of urgency" is an essential emotional hot button.

Intangible products: (Non-physical) Are bought for use at a future date, i.e., insurance, intellectual property, ideas, mortgages, blueprints. Like tangible, each intangible product's industry has a unique style of selling using differing "hot button" words, phrases and non-verbal communication. The vocabulary of intangible selling relies heavily on different sensory sections of the brain that controls emotional visualization.

An intangible product example: A realtor is selling a per-constructed home. As stated, intangible selling relies heavily on the salesperson's ability to paint mental pictures within the potential client's imagination.

1. The salesperson must be able to stand on different empty lots and allow the potential client to imagine the different house positions, the trees, shrubs, and flower placement. Then, looking at blueprints imagining the room sizes, who will get which bedroom? What will be in each bathroom? How will the kitchen look and how will the appliances fit?... Get the picture?

2. The urgency factor is also lower. Unlike the constructed, ready-to-sell home with competition by other realtors who could sell the house to another family, your potential client is deciding if they are prepared to buy. An un-built home's urgency factor is lower because it will take time to build, the potential client may need to pick a building lot, and it often takes more time to obtain and define construction financing before the building begins.

Selling intangibles takes more concentration skills in leading the buyer toward a sale because intangible features of the home must now occur in the buyers' minds. The salesperson must understand the importance of, and learn how to, paint mental pictures using tools provided that will allow the buyer the ability to visualize each feature of the product, how it works, and how it will enhance the potential client's lifestyle.

Chapter 7

Product Features

Primary and Secondary

This is a short paragraph but very important. Usually, people think of a product feature as the direct features that are built in to the product.

Primary features are essential for selling tangible products because the salesperson can demonstrate the features of the product while in the presentation, and for painting those mental pictures while selling intangibles.

The perceptive salesperson also uses secondary features. A secondary feature is an additional feature which is created by a benefit from/by a primary feature. Employing secondary features of a product can often be the edge the salesperson needs to make the sale.

An example of a secondary feature of a tangible product; purchasing a car. A person buys an older but certified used car versus a new car. One primary feature would be a lower purchase price. Two of the many secondary features of an older car with a lower purchase price would be lower insurance cost and lower registration license fees and/or excise tax.

An example of secondary features of an intangible product; purchasing a whole-life insurance policy. A whole life policy is issued at age 41 and has a provisional clause written within the policy that guarantees, from the issuance date, the annual premium will remain the same amount for the life of the insured "locked-in."

The primary feature is a locked-in annual premium. A secondary feature of life insurance is the proceeds are received "tax-free" to the beneficiary. The salesperson can paint mental pictures of possible future costs of cancer, heart disease, or other health issues, including the cost of final expenses being paid with "discounted" tax-free dollars often leaving 30% to 40% extra to the beneficiary, while an annuity or some retirement programs may be taxed at death. Knowing as many primary and secondary features that your product contains adds arrows to your sales quiver. To harvest your sale, use those arrows and shoot straight at your goal (the sale).

Space for Notes

SECTION 2
Preparation

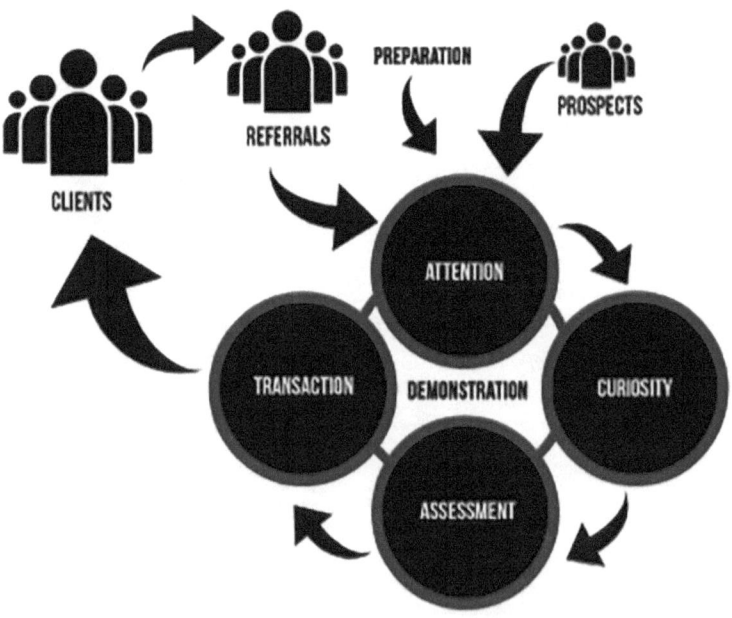

Chapter 8

Understanding Potential Clients

Surveys

After you have done your homework, preparation, and taken a deep breath, it's time you started becoming a professional salesperson. Over the last fifty years, there have been countless surveys by behavior scientists and psychotherapists studying potential clients' experiences with salespeople. These surveys cover a broad range of sales procedures from tele-marketing, business-to-business, inbound and outbound sales and various other techniques and methods.

Unfortunately, according to potential clients, the results were negative at every step of the sale, which culminated with these top four responses:

1. 69% wanted the salesperson to listen to their NEEDS.

2. 61% wanted more associated information.

3. 51% wanted the salesperson to respond promptly.

4. 61% didn't want the salesperson to be pushy.

And the surveys showed that over half of sales presentations had an adverse response. Think about it; over 50% negative.

The sales professional understands these statistics and quickly alters each category to promote variation in the sales presentation. Using the right and proper vocabulary, nonverbal communication, and the right tools, the professional can easily overcome obstacles, changing a potential client into a client.

Scientists and therapists also questioned new and average salespeople and asked them what, in their opinion, would increase their sales productivity. The top four results:

1. 42% wanted to raise the urgency to buy.

2. 35% wished to overcome money issues.

3. 28% wanted to close more deals.

4. 37% wanted to get in touch with more contacts.

A closer look at these stats reveals that the percentages of what the potential client wants from the salesperson were above 50%, yet the salesperson wants were under 45%!

The Daaaa Moment!!!

Logically, if the salesperson changes his/her presentation to satisfy the potential clients "wants" the salesperson will increase their sales ratio. Just as the professional quickly understood and changed his/her approach, the new or average salesperson can make changes. If the salesperson can decrease the potential client's negative issues by just 25% the salesperson's, negative problems are eliminated. The sales professional, new and average salespeople, are on equal ground, having established an advantage once the presentation begins.

The potential client confirms "when" to meet for a face-to-face presentation, the potential client knows the "why" of the meeting, "what" products will be offered, and there is a likely "need" for the product... The professional is also aware that even though each sales presentation is unique, potential clients have traits that the professional can categorize and be able to use as shortcuts in future sales situations.

By studying your potential clients, you will be able to lead them straight to a positive transaction (sale) and convince them it was their idea. It is fun and exciting being a top-notch sales professional.

Imagine seeing scores of potential clients and making more sales. The sales professional understands and uses this technique to build an ongoing sales career. Working smarter, not harder.

Space for Notes

Chapter 9

Words, Phrases, and Nonverbal Communication

Have you ever heard these expressions about the sales profession? "The successful sales professional uses words as a surgeon uses a scalpel." "Words and phrases are the tools of the salesperson." "Nonverbal actions can make or break a sale." "A sale is like building a house." "One word can lose a sale."

The backbone of any sale, even with all our technological advances in communication, are still primarily made with words, phrases, and nonverbal communication. These three communications components help in acting as a blueprint in building your sales style, painting mental pictures, activating the senses, stimulating your imagination, creating associations, mental distractions, and linking two or more things that wouldn't usually go together. Knowing and understanding your vocabulary will help you develop goals and habits.

A good goal and great confidence builder are knowing and understanding the words of your sales industry. Write down your industry's words on a legal pad. Understand that the more senses you use, seeing, hearing, speech, along with mentally visualizing each word as you write, will use multiple portions of the brain simultaneously, allowing you to recall each word or phrase quickly.

Words

Words are as varied as the building materials involved in building a house. The contractor hired to construct the house has the responsibility of finding and purchasing specific materials to be used, and needed, during specified times of construction. The contractor, for example, wouldn't have roofing shingles delivered while pouring cement for a basement. These materials, like the words of the sales procedure, are varied but necessary. Each has a specific function and need. Materials like nails, screws, cement, lumber, bricks, mortar, plaster, wallboard, paint, shingles, carpet, windows, appliances, furnace, air conditioning unit, and water heater.

When the house is completed and sold, the new owner brings in furniture and other articles to make a house into a home.

Just as the contractor finds and purchases (using many salespeople) the right materials in the right amounts and delivered at the right time to build a house, the salesperson must also find specific materials (words), among thousands, to use in the construction of a sale. Both contractor and salesperson understand the more exact the amounts and quality of materials/words used, the more potential profit.

Quality high ranking words are useful in all steps of the sales process. Therefore, the more you use correct wording within your calls, proposals, sales presentations, and with clients, the more you can have a perpetual sales career. It must be WARNED, however, that although high ranking words are powerful, they must be used under improper context and order to make sense to the contact/potential client/client. Just listing power words does not work.

- Persuasive words: Among 100s of high-ranking words are some common persuasive words like: own, imagine, love, health, save, safety, discovery, you, us, because, instantly, fast, immediately, fix, new, we. These words are very helpful in getting the prospect's attention, are personal, and so are useful in call-to-action, headlines, opening line sentences, emails, tweeter, websites, and transactions.

- Influential words are aligned with persuasive words and help in the mental visualization of the product's benefits, features, usefulness, and wants. Like persuasive words, there are 100s. Words like: approve, compare, introducing, easy, quick, feel, found, felt, offer, startling, miracle, magic, bargain, hurry, sensational, improvement, announcing, suddenly, wanted, challenge, remarkable, investment, presentation, and client. Influential and persuasive words are helpful in keeping the prospect interested in your product and increasing the want of your product.

There are also words that are better kept out of any conversation with a potential client.

- Negative words: It is essential to know certain words that can throw a negative cloud over your sales process. Remember, one word can blow a sale. Words like: problem, discount, contract, actually, competitor, (large numbers) million, billion, trillion, abstract, buy, prospects, hope, don't, obviously, quota, cheap, perhaps, cost, price, forbidden, sign, pitch, customers, honestly, maybe, stuff, opportunity, basic, and noise words like erm, uhm, ahh, OK.

Phrases

A phrase is a group (2-7) words that express an idea. Like words, phrases can help or hurt your sales style in developing a client. If your words and phrases are presented sloppily, your potential client is going to hear or read your words and unconsciously pick up the subject, not the content. You want your phrases to be direct and confident.

- Positive phrases include: shall we get started, the answer to your question is, thank you for your trust, allow me to show you, hearing your needs I feel your best next step would be this product, this product fills that void, thank you for allowing me to be your _____ professional. Hello, I'm calling back to set an appointment about our new quick and easy_____

You could also lose a sale using the wrong phrases just as using an incorrect word.

- Negative phrases include: sorry I bothered you, just checking in, trust me, what if I said, that's not what I meant, to be honest, touching base, could you direct me to the decision-maker, I'd like to have an informal chat, I need to, do you have a budget for this, so you're not interested in my product, actually, that's not true.

Each of these negative phrases, which most people use every day, can increase the chances of NO SALE.

Nonverbal Communication

Nonverbal communication: All communication that doesn't involve speech is nonverbal, and nearly two thirds of any discussion is applied non verbally. Author Peter F Drucker once stated, "the most important thing in communication is to hear what isn't said." Professional salespeople use nonverbal techniques to hold the attention, excitement, want, and trust in the sales call presentation and transaction. The following are nonverbal procedures that are essential to your professional sales career: facial expressions, the tone of voice, body movement, physical appearance, eye contact, gestures, posture, silence placed, and time.

Take a moment and imagine your last failed face-to-face meeting. Remember how the potential client looked (inattentive or drifting), what they did (fidgety, looking around), how they were listening (silent, not understanding), and what they were doing (doodling, squirming, looking down). Nonverbal communication can tell you what your contact or potential client is thinking even over the phone.

Learning how to use words, phrases, and nonverbal communication helps not only you with calls and potential clients. Another essential nonverbal communication is the ability to listen to your inner voice; keeping it positive. All too often we let our inner voice direct our daily routines. As you are reading this book, you are using your inner voice to understand, the words as written, metaphors and analogies, while practicing your visualization skills. Use your inner voice to practice your calls and presentations beforehand, to help correct flaws while increasing positive habits, confidence, peace-of-mind, excitement, and more sales will be your reward.

Space for Notes

Chapter 10

Contact Calls-Scripts

Separating the grain from the chaff involves toil and time. Contact calls involve: practice, time, accomplishment joy, pain, and rejection. Plan on spending 60% of your weekly duties making contact calls. According to Brevet, "92% of all customer interactions happen over the phone." I recommend 80% of initial contact calls between Tuesday and Thursday, 9:00 am to 4:30 pm. If you want more success, whether new to the sales industry or a veteran, the contact call is the starting line.

Cold calling: The new salesperson gets chills when hearing "cold call." Maybe that's how it got its name? Another reason could be the idea that the new salesperson knows little about who they are calling. Some websites and blogs proclaim that the cold call is dead. I can't entirely agree. With all the technology at our disposal, we have the opportunity to evaluate a contact before placing the call.

Today, let's use the term "warm calling." You can send an email, Instagram, Twitter, see them on a social site, or read their profile on sites like LinkedIn, or in a company directory. Ask yourself, "where" did you get this so-called call? "Why" are you calling this set of prospects? "What" sets them apart from random names out of a phone book? Knowing the where, why, what reasons will give you confidence that you already have an edge, and this edge is all that is needed to be successful. "When" you master the "warm calling," your sales career is set for life.

The sales professional has learned to feel the contact's first impressionable sounds within a call and obtains the contact's attention by having an alert and clear voice. (No one wants to hear a smoker's cough or cares if you were up all night with a sick child.) I found, in my years selling, the following "call-scripts" were very effective with "warm calls", no matter the product.

- Introduce yourself and company—and for God's sake don't say "how are you today?" or "how are you doing?" say "hello Mr./Ms. _____ my name is_____ and I represent _____." (Think like a professional and go right into why you called.) "I called to make an appointment to show you our new, quick and easy_____, because I feel you might want to see for yourself the benefits the _____ has to offer." Now shut up and let the contact speak first, and whatever they say, answer truthfully. If they say, "OK fine," make an appointment. If the questions continue, SAY "the answer to your question is_____" then say, "Allow me to show you, what is your best time?" and make the appointment.

- If they say NO to your call, don't feel pain quite yet. Say "some of my clients felt the same way when I first called them." "I had to gain their trust, and if you feel the same, may I call you back in two weeks?" Alternatively, you could say "I understand, some of my clients felt the same way. I understand because things can change, so may I call you back in 3 weeks?" Most of the time they will say yes just to get you off the phone. Now make a firm time and date. Say, "I will call you at 5:43 pm on Wednesday, Sept. 12 Mr./Ms. _____ talk with you then, thank you and bye." Note: There is a reason to make an odd callback time. You will understand when reading the GOLD File section.

Response to an ad: These types of calls are easy to turn into sales calls because like order taking, the contact contacts you. These contacts are usually done with emails, texts or a mailer. You have the advantage because you have their pertinent information ahead of your sales call, and you know they are already interested in your products.

- Say, "hello Mr./Ms._____. I received your response to our advertisement about our new quick and easy _____. I called to make an appointment so that I might show you the many features available to you and your family." Now follow the same steps as the "warm call" for setting the appointment.

Curiosity response: These types of contacts are information seekers. Making the presentation is rather easy, but be prepared, because curiosity callers want you to answer lots of questions over the phone. So when you call:

- Say, "hello Mr./Ms. _____ I received your response to our advertisement for our new quick and easy _____. I called to make an appointment so that I might show you the many features available to you and your family." When they start to ask questions, say "I understand you have lots of questions like many of my current clients did, and that is exactly why I want to show you and answer each one. Allow me the opportunity. What is your best time?" (Make the appointment.)

Also, understand you will spend lots of time, and obtaining a sale is below average. However, don't make the mistake of canceling. Because if you make these types of contact calls into clients, they will give you tons of quality referrals.

Add-ons and repeat purchases: The most accessible form of a sales call. Just be friendly and thankful and make a date for a SALE.

Referrals: Anyone that will allow you to use their name to promote you and your product, i.e., clients, friends, neighbors, business acquaintances, individual search engines; all offer credibility to your professionalism. Referrals are why businesses use well-known personalities to sell the product. Obtaining a sales presentation is made more accessible, and the positive transaction rate is around 80%.

- Say, "Hello Mr./Ms. _____, my name is_____, and I represent _____. Your name was given to me by your friend and my client _____. She has the trust and confidence in me to refer you, because she felt you would enjoy seeing our new, quick and easy_____. I'm therefore calling to make an appointment, what is the best time for you?" If they say NO, use my GOLD File.

Space for Notes

Chapter 11

My Gold File

I'm sure you have heard of the "Law of Large Numbers" theory. In sales, it means the more calls you make, the more people you see, the higher your success. I say: Nonsense!!! An examination of initial contact calls reveals less than 10% will respond favorably, leaving 90% to say no. Without the right tools, the right attitude, and the proper knowledge, you could call hundreds of people, waste time and go broke.

Earlier in this chapter, we described how to improve your "call scripts" to increase sales presentations and raise your closing ratio, and we discussed how 92% of sales are transacted over the phone. Now, I want to explain my Gold File and show how using it will make you bunches of money.

I developed the Gold File (named for the extra money it makes) when working for Metropolitan Life Insurance Co. The Gold File was instrumental in helping me move up the ranks from agent to sales manager to Advanced Underwriting Adviser to General Manager while qualifying for the Million Dollar Round Table.

My GOLD File was designed to capture a percentage of NO responses from your initial contact calls and turn them into sales. The Gold File can extract about 45% of NO responses and add them to the "yes" column.

As stated earlier, start by collecting all NO responses and keep a detailed profile, including their response to any previous correspondence, on your device or card file of every contact call made.

In chapter 10, I gave you the following script. I feel its importance bears repeating.

•   Say, "Some of my clients felt the same way when I first called them." "I had to gain their trust, and if you feel the same, may I call you back in two weeks?" Alternatively, you could say "I understand, some of my clients felt the same way. I understand because things can change, so may I call you back in 3 weeks?" Most of the time they will say yes just to get you off the phone. Now make a firm time and date. Say "I will call you at 5:43 pm on Wednesday, Sept. 12 Mr./Ms. _____, talk with you then, thank you and bye" to all calls made that you can call back at a specific time and date. Always make the call at a time that falls on an odd minute, i.e., 5:13, 6:27, or 4:33.

Odd appointment times do three things.

1. It makes the contact wonder why such an odd callback time (by being odd it will help "pin" their future memory).

2. At precisely the time and date you set, call. Now you will have kept a promise (building trust and confidence with the contact for you).

3. It shows you value his/her business. It might take a few calls to make a sales presentation, but as the year goes forward you will be gathering future clients and valuable referrals from an initial NO most salespeople discard.

For every initial NO, the Gold File extracts over 60% to become potential clients, and surprisingly, 80% of those will become clients (sales). Who said, "you can't make something from nothing."

Chapter 12

Mechanics of a Presentation

The Sales Presentation

The sales presentation is a culmination of all prior work the salesperson has performed, understanding the rotating selling phases, and knowing the formation and structure of each phase.

With some 40 years of selling gobs of different tangible and intangible products while reading hundreds of blogs, websites, training manuals, watching numerous videos, and attending countless seminars concerning sales presentations, selling phases, and cycles (even writing and teaching many of them), I understand they come in all sizes and varieties, i.e., psychological, sociological, hard, and soft. If used correctly, these bountiful forms can be productive.

I also know a little secret that I would like to share with my readers, and this is an excellent time to reveal that secret... "No matter which emotional or psychological platform you decide to use, you will be more profitable by using the GOLD File and these four very distinct, effective and rotating phases: Attention, Curiosity, Assessment, Transaction. Simple and easy.

These phases form a perpetual rotating motion of selling that creates subtle pressure, which holds the salesperson and the potential client captive, like centrifugal force, moving the presentation closer and closer to a positive transaction (sale).

Caution: Dropping, not fully completing, forgetting, or moving too fast through any one phase can distort the presentation causing it to "fly apart" with respect to time line, momentum, and control.

When or if a phase is violated, don't get discouraged. Start the rotation over at the Attention phase. This doesn't mean you repeat yourself, but instead, use the rotating motion to your advantage to get back on track. Remember, the sales professional controls the presentation, so it rotates and flows smoothly from each phase on to the next.

Don't group too many questions at the beginning or end, but rather spread questions throughout the presentation. This will help to make it more of a natural conversation rather than an "interview" or "sales pitch."

Just imagine a cutting board, and on it, there is a teaspoon of sugar, a pinch of cinnamon, a teaspoon of fresh ground coffee, a tablespoon of flavored cream, and a cup of clean water. Look at it from a couple of different angles. All the things needed to make a nice cup of coffee. However, to thoroughly enjoy that cup of coffee, you need to follow a finite order: Heat the water, then pour the hot water into a cup. Now, in order, add in the teaspoon of coffee, a teaspoon of sugar, a tablespoon of flavored cream, and a pinch of cinnamon. Then thoroughly stir. Mmmm, now you have a great cup of coffee; you can taste, smell, and even feel the goodness.

Heating up your presentation with prior work performed, adding the phases in their predetermined order and stirring with a rotating motion will give you a satisfied client, A SALE, and referrals.

Attention Phase

So as they say, "we have come to where the rubber meets the road." You've done your homework, made your calls, set your appointment, prepared a proposal, got all gussied up, arrived on time, annnnnd "HELLO Mr./Ms. _____," a firm handshake, while looking eye-to-eye with a positive nonverbal facial expression and gestures. NOW, you have about 15 seconds to get your potential client's attention fixated on you.

Tip: People always like to talk about themselves, their hobbies and prized possessions. If you are in the potential client's home or office, take a quick look around. Do you see anything thought-provoking? A sports trophy, painting, jewelry, flowering plants, animals, music system, display, antiques, car, anything your potential client would be proud to spend an hour in explanation?

If you're in your office or a neutral place, look to see if your potential client has any unusual or expensive outer clothing, i.e., glasses, coat, gloves, hat, shoes or boots, purse, jewelry, or a cute hairdo, cell phone, tattoos, briefcase. Even if only a notebook or legal pad you can start by saying, "I am glad you came prepared to take some notes. It shows your thoroughness."

The Attention phase is where you start building a relationship and moving toward a professional/client bond. To further strengthen this bond, begin to entwine your experiences with similar stories the potential client tells, but never try and one-up your potential client. Always let them have the better stories.

Once you have the potential client's attention, start to rotate the conversation toward the next phase by using eye-to-eye contact and focusing on the proposal and the features of the product. Work on transition, but never hurry the potential client. Stay interested in what he/she is saying.

Start to move the conversation by mastering the nonverbal skill of silence placing, (knowing where to insert silence in your presentation) and using this sales technique frequently. This technique is so powerful the potential client will often help move the conversation for you. They might abruptly say, "so what have you got to show me?" or "Is that paperwork for me?" even "well, let's see what-ja got there." These statements, as well as yours, like, "let me show you the new features available, for you and your family, on this latest model" or "let us imagine this beautiful addition to your garage," will rotate the presentation forward.

Curiosity Phase

The curiosity phase is the "grabbing" phase of the presentation. In this phase your product and its features take center stage. The Curiosity Phase answers <u>the one challenging key question that every potential client must satisfy if you are to obtain a sale: "Will it benefit me?" (VALUE)</u>

Many sales platforms teach logical programs to find a motive for why people buy things, and salespeople are taught many of them, like: avoidance, pain, fear, feel important, health, be secure, comfortable, be liked, pride, gain knowledge. Motives help in a presentation and are referred to as "help reasons." I even found a blog that has "100 reasons why people buy stuff"-wow- imagine that presentation! All these reasons eventually lead to this one key question, "Will it benefit me?" So, concentrate on this key question, "will it benefit me?" Make sales simple and easy.

Give the product value. I would recommend, in preparation for the presentation, that you write out 5 or more features your product can deliver to the potential client that will make his/her lifestyle better. Using the product, design your presentation in a way that the potential client will ask questions concerning the primary and secondary features. Encourage lots of questions. Remember, the more questions your potential client requests, the more you can enforce "will it benefit me" and continued bonding.

Always answer each question truthfully. Don't know the answer? Be truthful. SAY "how important is that in your decision?" If it is not that important, then say, "I will find out when I'm back at the office and call you with the answer." Make certain you call. If the question could be a deal breaker, say, "well, I don't see that in my notes. Let me call my manager. Give me a minute. I'll find out." Give the potential client something to read while you call so he/she will not lose attention. It is your responsibility to let the potential client know that their questions are important and will be answered.

Be disciplined in this phase. Use stories of your current clients who have benefited from your product. Use metaphors and analogies (like the coffee one I used earlier); they are great tools because they focus the potential client's mental visualization skills and energizes his/her senses.

During this phase try not to use certain words, i.e., guarantee, seriously, basically, or problem. Never use the words cheap, quota, hope or noise words like erm, mmm, ahh, OK. These words and noises are unnerving to the potential clients during this phase because they show the salesperson's unpreparedness...

Back to questions. When talking about the features of your product or answering your potential client's questions, start by saying, "Here's what will benefit you" and end with "and that's value." These two sentences will help encapsulate your responses, focusing the potential clients on his key question. You want the potential client to be satisfied that he/she is getting value, and repetition is an effective sales method.

This phase is also the place to start using ABC (always be closing). If the potential client asks, "Is this appliance self-cleaning?" answer, "Yes, I suggest you run the self-cleaning feature as soon as it is delivered before you use it, and we can have it set up in your home next Tuesday."

Assessment Phase

As you sense the potential client is satisfying his value questions, and even wanting the product as the above example illustrates, rotate the cycle into the assessment phase. This phase can be short and go directly to the transaction or, if the potential client has doubts about the product and features, this phase will be where money takes center stage. It is at this stage that the potential client is thinking, "am I getting more than the purchase price" (show me the value, and I'll show you the money); emotional responses are heavily relied upon in this phase.

Consider the Assessment phase as the fortifying stage that connects you and the potential client to the product and starts the change from potential client to client. I like to think of it as the butterfly phase. Imagine, just as the butterfly twists and turns to free him/herself from the cocoon revealing its beauty and grace, the potential client is also trying to shrug off past adverse events and lack of knowledge that may have created a focus on the purchase price (money) more than the benefits of the product.

The salesperson must understand the value of their products and features and convey how they outweigh the purchase price. The salesperson must use this knowledge to neutralize any past adverse events and then bring the potential client forward, in a step-by-step motion, while offering the data necessary to allow the potential client to imagine the benefits offsetting the purchase price, all while looking into his/her future use of the product. If the potential client is still fixated on the purchase price, you may want to reduce the purchase price into smaller sums. Also called, "reduce to the ridiculous."

Let's say an investment of $45,000 is required to remodel a kitchen. The potential client is somewhat satisfied with the features but has sticker shock. To help move the presentation forward, and show the benefits outweigh the purchase price, let us look at the secondary features. You might say: "Mr./Mrs. Your investment, over the next ten years for your kitchen remodel is about $86/wk." "$86/wk. for the most significant room that will add resale value to your home," "$86/wk. for the most impressive room in your home that friends and family will admire," "$86/wk. for the most important room in your home that will add safety and warmth in your home—the kitchen." "Just imagine your new appliances, that double stove." "Smell the bread and turkey baking simultaneously." "The new counter area close to the refrigerator and double depth stainless steel sinks. All for $86/wk." "We can schedule the start in two weeks on Wednesday." "Would you like to take advantage of our 90 days same as cash savings or our monthly investment plan?"

Notice I repeatedly used $86 dollars never mentioning $45,000. Also, the words we, us, investment value, admire, safety warmth, imagine, appeal to the money purchase price being offset by the product's features and additional emotional benefits; pride, love, wellness, and call to action.

Transaction Phase

As you can see from the example, we used the ABC and closed the sale in the assessment phase. However, the Transaction phase is still vital. As you read further, you will understand its importance. I use the term Transaction Phase rather than "the close" because it is an opening for the salesperson/client relationship.

CAUTION: The transaction phase is not always fruitful. As stated in chapter 3, there are three outcomes in this phase; positive transaction (sale), an agreed second or even third appointment (sale on hold), and a negative transaction (no sale). How you have rotated through every previous step will determine your outcome.

The professional salesperson instinctively can feel if the transaction phase seems to be leaning towards the negative. the professional also knows it will be necessary to continue rotating the selling motion back to the Attention phase and then further to the Curiosity and Assessment phases focusing the potential client's two most fundamental questions: "Will it benefit me?" and "Am I getting more than purchase price?" (VALUE and MONEY)

Once you have the potential client thinking positive, this phase is then devoted to cleaning up all the loose ends, collecting the purchase price or the first installment on an agreed payment plan, signing any paperwork, (the sale), and asking for referrals.

The professional salesperson will benefit not only from the sales of a product but also from the referrals received. Approximately 65% of clients are willing to offer referrals, but only 11% of salespeople ask. Earlier I recommended at least seven referrals as a start. Don't be too pushy concerning referrals. It may even be necessary to contact the client by phone or email to give time for your client to offer. Think of referrals as a tip for doing good work—get referrals.

Having a mature salesperson/client bond will, for years after, be able to cultivate a relationship. Even if your sale is a one-and-done, staying in touch with your "client base" will reap many rewards. Remember, a referral contact results in an appointment ratio of close to 60% with a positive transaction ratio of over 80% (money in the bank).

Space for Notes

Chapter 13

Bringing It All Together

Whether contemplating a sales career, new to the sales industry, or a seasoned veteran, making sales is the name of the game. As in the sports world, fans don't care about the long hours you practice or your knowledge of your sport. They only care if you win. In the sales industry, it's sales that prove you are a winner.

How to Build a Professional Sales Career is designed in two sections. The Preparation section gave insight into the necessary building blocks of job security, eliminating the garbage, energy building through vocabulary performance, sales rules, goals, habits, types of products, and product features, along with prior educational accomplishments. The Demonstration section took the confidence built from earlier chapters and created a successful step-by-step direct sales procedure. These include: the potential client/client relationship, verbal and nonverbal communication, calls and scripts, and the phases of the continuous rotating motion of the presentation. I have also included my GOLD File as an addition to your sales call ratio.

Just as a playwright uses props along with communication skills to offer a memorable story, the successful salesperson develops the ability to paint mental pictures using proposals and communication, showing that their product enhances the client's lifestyle.

If along the way the reader gained just one idea and focuses your presentation towards "will it benefit me?" (value) and "am I getting more than I'm giving up?" (money), you will see a marked increase in your bottom line—more sales.

This Book will increase your ability to become a professional salesperson in any business where sales products are for sale, from business-to-business to one-on-one contact. Use this Book regularly to sharpen your sales skills, and you will be successful in any sales industry you desire. Salespeople are in high demand and will remain that way as long as there are products to sell.

....

I would personally appreciate a moment of your time to write a review. It might also help a new salesperson to become a sales professional.

Please visit my website www.richardlericksoncht.com and watch for future publications.

www.ingramcontent.com/pod-product-compliance
Lightning Source LLC
Chambersburg PA
CBHW021042180526
45163CB00005B/2247